DISRUPTED!

DISRUPTED!

How to Create the Future When the Old Rules are Broken

Philippa Hardman
&
Chris Nichols

Matador
9 Priory Business Park,
Wistow Road, Kibworth Beauchamp,
Leicestershire. LE8 0RX
Tel: 0116 279 2299
Email: books@troubador.co.uk
Web: www.troubador.co.uk/matador
Twitter: @matadorbooks

ISBN 978 1 80046 040 9

British Library Cataloguing in Publication Data.
A catalogue record for this book is available from the British Library.

Printed and bound in the UK by 4edge Limited
Typeset in 11pt Adobe Jenson Pro by Troubador Publishing Ltd, Leicester, UK

Matador is an imprint of Troubador Publishing Ltd

To our past, present and future clients,
with whom all of this is developed
and through whom the world is changed.

CONTENTS

INTRODUCTION

We've spent twenty years as agents of disruption.

We've annoyed boards. We've been thrown out of organisations. We've fired clients.

But we've stuck at our work. We felt we had no choice. We saw that the multiple systems on which life depends were failing. So we've spent our time working with people, in many sectors, who saw the same thing and who became determined to rise to the creative challenge that this posed in their personal lives and in how they affected their organisations.

We've not become famous. No TED talks, no bestsellers. We have a niche, award-winning consulting practice doing work with executive teams, individual leaders and, through them, their organisations. Clients describe the approaches we use with them as provocative, challenging and ultimately very practical. We like to think we've made, and are still making, a real difference.

When we decided to put down in writing what we've learnt, and taught, over those years, we couldn't find a publisher who wanted the book as we'd created it. They wanted two books. They wanted a different book. We wanted to write *this* book. It's short, it's straightforward and people need it right now. So, we've published it ourselves instead.

We dedicate this book to all the amazing people we have met and worked with in that time. And to everyone who picks it up, trying to address the multiple crises and systems challenges that we now face as a species.

Philippa Hardman & Chris Nichols
May 2020

1 THE KNIFE EDGE

We live in a time of crisis.

There are plenty of books on how to manage in such times. This is not one of those. It's not about how to handle the first weeks of chaos; it's about how to come out of the crisis with full focus on creating a new future, not simply replaying the game plan that led to the broken systems in the first place. It's a book for real leaders in real organisations: the people who have to reboot and reinvent the systems that are broken. If they don't do it, no-one else can.

Given that it's obvious that everyone needs to become better at working with the unknown in a world of perpetual disruption, won't this change 'just happen'? Well, maybe, and maybe not. There's a lot of imposed change just waiting to spring back into deep patterns (the world can't afford that) and there's a lot of inertia coiled and waiting to preserve those patterns. Inertia must not be allowed to win the day.

Organisations can get stuck – sooner than they think. They have structures, identities, processes: ways of being, ways of doing, ways of learning. These give rise to how the people within them see, hear and experience the world. They give rise to how people develop positions about all kinds of things, including strategies, campaigns, initiatives, stakeholder relationships, products, brands, systems, profit margins, organisational identity, culture, go-to markets and must-win battles.

Organisations become big, powerful and successful. They become known for being great at this or for having an unrivalled capacity for that. People want to join them. People in the organisation pour their energy into supporting and reinforcing these things. They fit in, get promoted, earn more money and acquire fancy titles.

All of this can work brilliantly, right up to the moment when the world becomes critically different to the world as it was. At this point, which occurs before anyone thinks there is any kind of crisis, the organisation needs to see those changes and respond. There is a moment – we call it a 'knife edge' – where all the great components of past success become threats to future flourishing. They start to entice the leader, the team, the whole organisation into *not* seeing, into *not* changing.

This book tells you how to stop this happening. It is full of practical ways to see more clearly, to free up stuck thinking and action, and to allow more flourishing to develop, so that your organisation learns to swim in the current of change. The alternative is decline, often slow to start with, but, also often, dramatic at the end.

The crowded horizon

Change is everywhere. Most of you will have a strong sense that there are a lot of powerful and important shifts going on in the world: ones that are filled with threats, but also opportunities. This is the stuff of the 'horizon scanning' that business planners and strategy gurus want us all to focus on.

They're right. It's worth taking a look at just some of the major changes that are (or should be) on the agenda of every organisation. The current and all-pervading virus pandemic is the most visible of these factors right now (and every organisation and every government is working out what to do as a result). But coronavirus is just the latest manifestation of failure in a complex inter-connected tangle of systems in crisis. It may be the most immediate difficulty we all have to deal with, but it will not be the last and it isn't separate from many of the other huge challenges that are looming on our shared horizons.

The digital re-invention of everything

Business and work life is being, and will be, deeply affected by the impact of these chaotic times, and by the reorganisations and reinventions forced on society.

It seems that a reluctant world has just taken a deep dive into a massive digital shift. People who had never used an app are suddenly part of webs of virtual communities: from online Buddhist centres to doctors doing video consultation as a standard offer; from instant global sharing of expertise among clinical teams to open source patents for 3D printed ventilators. Suddenly everyone seems fully bought in to the digital reinvention of the future.

When the virus crisis is over, will things 'ping' back to conditions as they once were? We think not.

Many people have felt the huge relief of a different way of working and will want more of it. Many will now be sceptical about the hyper-mobility of jetting around the world to team up with colleagues face-to-face. We sense there has been a catalytic moment in the realisation of the digital age. But where does it go from here? What will business look like after this immediate crisis passes? That is all to be created, and everyone will be involved in the process.

The identities of every organisation, and the people within them, will have to shift in response to these challenges. Are we ready? The world needs a whole new passion for constant re-learning, everywhere and always in organisational life. This is not about telling people what the digital future is – no one knows yet. It is more like Antoine de Saint-Exupéry's notion: "If you want to build a ship, don't drum up men to gather wood and give orders … instead, teach them to yearn for the vast and endless sea."

The great global gamble

The virus is just part of a bigger shift in human reality. Everyone knows about the climate crisis, but human impact on the planet is adversely affecting its ability to sustain life in more ways than that. In 2008, Johan Rockström, Director of the Stockholm Resilience Centre (SRC), led a group of internationally recognised scientists who identified and quantified nine processes that regulate the stability of Earth's ecosystem. They are:

- *Loss of biosphere diversity and increase in extinctions*: the evidence is clear that human activity is diminishing the diversity of life on the planet, with a big increase in impact over the most recent 50 years.
- *Land use change*: human use of ever greater areas of land for agriculture, industry and cities has a global as well as local effect. The shift is from diverse vegetation, such as forests, grasslands and wetlands, to a more standard agricultural or industrial pattern, which contributes to biodiversity loss, impacts freshwater cycles and concentrates pollution.
- *Chemical pollution and the release of 'novel entities'*: our ingenuity in creating new chemicals has resulted in more, and new, forms of waste, some of which damage the environment in ways not yet fully understood.
- *Atmosphere aerosol loading*: airborne particle numbers are rising and are dangerous. About 800,000 deaths a year are calculated to be linked to such forms of pollution.
- *Ocean acidification*: about 25% of the carbon dioxide released by human activity ends up dissolved in the seas, where it becomes carbonic acid. The more acidic the water, the harder it is for some sea creatures to make their skeletons and shells. This runs a risk of changing the food chain in the seas,

with huge knock-on consequences for other species – including humans.

- *Freshwater use and hydrological cycles*: fresh water is obviously vital to human life, and is becoming scarce. By 2050 half a billion people will be living without adequate access to water.
- *Nitrogen and phosphorus flows*: agricultural and chemical processes have damaged these natural flows. The chemical run-offs usually end up in watercourses and impact the oxygenation of rivers and coastal seas.
- *Ozone depletion*: ozone in the atmosphere protects us from radiation and skin cancer. Action has already been taken on this one and the levels now seem to be stable and within safe limits.
- *Climate change*: the effect is evident, but the big question now is how much tolerance there is before shifts become rapid and irreversible.

This work proposed limits in each of these processes, within which human life can flourish. Any significant breach of these boundaries raises the risk of catastrophic, sudden, irreversible changes.

A recent update showed that human activity has now breached four of these: climate change, biodiversity loss, nitrogen flows and land use.

These conclusions present all of us, whether in business or in other forms of social and organisational life, with huge challenges – but also with astonishing opportunities to take a new direction. The invitation for innovation is endless, from lower emission transportation to better food production, from super-efficient manufacturing to innovative chemicals that do not harm living cycles.

The demographic shifts

In 1950 around 250 million people worldwide were over 60. Today it's closer to 1 billion, and by 2050 it is set to reach 2 billion. By 2100 it will be about a third of the total population. In some places the figures are even starker. In Japan the over 65 age group already makes up 26% of the total and this is expected to top 40% by 2050. In Europe the over 65s are closer to 19%, with the share of the population over 80 set to increase sharply by 2050.

This changing shape of the world population presents a whole raft of challenges and opportunities. How will health and welfare systems cope with such a growing group of people, with all the long-term healthcare needs that aging brings? Who will provide social care for this population? Some of the innovation opportunities are obvious, such as the search for treatments for dementia and solutions to mobility issues. Could social care be provided by robots or other forms of machine intelligence?

Population isn't just changing 'shape', it is increasing. In the decades ahead, the world will have to feed an ever-growing number of people without squandering increasingly scarce energy resources or creating waste. What kind of farming will we need? Will the world require a massive shift into laboratory-designed foods to take animals (and all of their suffering and carbon costs) totally out of the human food chain? Will environmental pressures put a cap on the use of agricultural use of chemical fertilisers? Will superbug resistance drive an eradication of the use of antibiotics in the food system?

How will this population be provided with energy? Will there be a renaissance of nuclear power? Will the world find new and more reliable ways to tap sufficient energy from the sun, waves, wind and other renewable sources? Will we drive cars? Will we fly? Will communities have to be redesigned around low energy, local employment and amenities? Or will new technologies be created to allow a super low-impact version of today's way of life to continue?

The New Politics

The very richest 1% now own over 50% of the world's wealth, and the gap between rich and poor is growing. An economic model that drives such inequality may turn out to have limited political support. What does this mean for the type of companies we have? Where are they based, how do they structure themselves, and how do they trade and pay their taxes? All of these questions are looming in boardrooms around the world and they are a long way from being resolved.

Inequality has led, many argue, to an increase in populism in politics, with the rise of nationalism and the emergence of archetypal 'strong-man' leaders who offer to bring justice to those who feel disenfranchised by the global economy. These leaders call for a rejection of the post-war frameworks of globalisation and free trade, and for more intervention to protect national markets. They have little enthusiasm for trans-national organisations such as the UN or the EU.

It is an intriguing thought that, with the rise of nationalist governments, many of which seem determined to ignore international political bodies and to be unconcerned with transnational issues like climate change, multi-national companies (and NGOs) may end up as the only organisations with a combination of real power and a genuinely global perspective. These companies will be forced to take action on the big issues because, despite complaints about corporate short-termism, they have a longer view than that of ratings-chasing populist politicians. Climate catastrophe would be disastrous for business – and for everything else.

The challenges listed above are huge – and only a sample of the issues facing us in the future. We prefer to see them as huge opportunities – but almost no-one in any organisation that we know is really on top of this. Don't they care? We know people who do, passionately. But their organisations get in the way. Why?

The problem with problems

One argument used by those unwilling to deal with these issues is that they are simply 'too difficult'. They get shut away in drawers, often labelled 'VUCA'.

What does that label mean?

VUCA is an acronym for any situation that has the following characteristics: volatility, uncertainty, complexity and ambiguity. The word was dreamed up by the US military, and has come into frequent business use (though not always in a helpful way).

The VUCA label gets a lot of criticism, often being seen as a bit of a fad. That may be right. But it does remind us to take a close look at some things that do really matter. We are particularly concerned with two of the four VUCA factors, uncertainty and complexity.

Uncertainty is nothing new: everything in the world lies on a continuum between the known and the unknown, and always has.

However, there is a lot of pressure in organisations to pretend that uncertainty doesn't exist and to create false certainties instead. Investors demand forecasts; the corporate centre calls for detailed plans; the capital allocation process requires estimates of market share and profit margin before a product even exists. It can be very hard to say, "I don't know." Power in organisations plays heavily into this. Many false certainties are created because someone in power requires certainty, or at least the illusion of it.

By contrast, uncertainty invites everyone to ask, "How do we know this is the case?" It invites us all to find out what we do know and to be brutal in our honesty about what we don't know. It invites us to make rigorous exploration of the unknowns. Some things are unknown but potentially knowable. Other things are more intrinsically unknown; a more rigorous knowledge of them cannot become available with the level of analysis that is available to us. So we must find better ways of investigating them, rather than falling back on helplessness or false ideas.

Positive disruptors embrace unknowing (we stress 'positive': this book isn't about destruction, but about ways to help organisations adapt, thrive and shape a better future). Embracing unknowing is not the same as celebrating ignorance. It's a frank admission that there are some things we just don't know yet. Unknowing provides an anvil against which to break down bullshit and the blind-sight of common assumptions, and motivates us to get serious about finding out some new things.

Complexity describes a state where cause and influence are interconnected and non-linear, and thus to some extent, unknown or unpredictable because the pattern, direction and magnitude of the causation is continually in flux.

Complexity is often confused with complication. These are not the same at all, and confusion over this lies at the heart of much that is awry in organisations.

- An Airbus 380 has four million parts. However, every time Airbus tries to make one, they get one. It never turns out to be something unexpected. That's because a jet is *complicated.* It has been designed. The function of each part is understood, as is the relationship between all those parts. It exists to operate within a range of tolerances. It takes a huge amount of planning and expertise to make one, but because it is complicated, it can be engineered.
- A management team is *complex.* The relationship between the parts is not linear and is unstable. People turn up in different ways, learn, develop,

change their minds, make unexpected decisions, and so the team shifts. This isn't collapsible to a replicable formula that always gives you a great management team.

One of the most common ways in which organisations address complex issues is to create complicated structures. But you can't do this – it's the wrong level of analysis. You might have the temporary comfort of thinking that you've contained the complex situation, but the reality is that you haven't. It's a false security, creating an illusion of imagining you're more sure of something than you really can be. It's a comfort blanket.

Nearly all of the challenges and opportunities highlighted in the previous section have some of the characteristics of VUCA challenges. But this does not make them impossible. They are invitations to do better work in system-shifting ways. The rewards could be huge.

Leading on the edge

The rest of this book is full of practices and perspectives to help you address challenges like these with confidence. As you do so, you'll be stepping away from the straight-line, certainty-based types of leadership and moving towards more alert, responsive approaches, which place exploring, experimentation and learning at their heart.

There's been a lot of theoretical writing over the years about how leaders can do this, often under the term 'adaptive leadership' or the 'learning organisation'. We will certainly allude to this, but our essential focus is on the practice – and on *you* as the practitioner. We will show you the tools and approaches that we have found most useful in doing this work.

This is work that starts paying dividends right away. Every step you take improves the contribution you'll make to your team and your organisation. You will add ever more value. You will have more satisfaction and resilience. And there's every chance of the world becoming better for it.

Let the work begin.

2 DO IT!

You want to play your part in positively disrupting your organisation. You are going to need new ways of working to achieve this. These will rest on two really important foundations: that you care enough to get involved and that you actually do something. Organisations aren't disrupted by words alone.

Care

To reinvent something, you have to care about it enough to bother. It's famously said that Richard Branson pretty much only enters markets where something has annoyed him: airlines, condoms, lotteries. Where he feels some pain, he sees a potential product.

We feel the same. Between us, we have spent over half a century in businesses and organisations, and we care about the potential for organisations of all kinds to be better than they are. We know just how much of their lives people pour into their work. It really matters to us that this time and life-energy is well placed and well used. We know that it is possible to change the top-down management and command-and-control styles that still dominate in many environments – and we have seen the amazing results that come about when, instead, human potential is unleashed to create wonderful workplaces. Better organisations, we believe, carry the seeds of a better world.

It's the same story for every one of the many great positive disruptors we've worked with. There is a fire in their belly about something, and they are prepared to put in the effort to address it.

Do you have this, too?

Action

Caring really matters, but it isn't enough. Having decided that you care enough about challenging and shifting something, you actually have to do something about it. Having a fire in your belly and then taking no action causes chronic indigestion.

Once you decide to take action, what will help you do it well?

The rest of this chapter guides you through a set of practices and perspectives that we know to be powerful and valuable. They've been part of our work for two decades. They provide a method and ideas that anyone can learn to use, and that start to pay dividends from day one of practice. We've divided them up as follows:

- Beyond certain: the Navigate-Explore model of the world

- Mastering exploration:
  - Start positive: take an appreciative stance
  - Invite and participate
  - Pay attention to the impact of your actions
  - Look wider, look deeper
  - Expect the unexpected & keep learning
- A disciplined approach to bring it all together
- Sustaining yourself in the work

Let's get cracking.

Beyond certain: the Navigate-Explore model of the world

This is a cornerstone for us.

In just about every kind of organisational work, it is really important to acknowledge that some things are more certain and predictable than others. We draw on a simple analogy to help get this thinking clearer. We call it the 'Navigate-Explore' framework. It has two zones.

The *Navigation zone* is when things are relatively stable and familiar, when you're dealing with technical issues (even demanding ones) and your existing experience and expertise is a good guide for action. We call it Navigation because you already have a good enough 'map' to guide the actions you need to take. Navigation tasks may be lengthy and complicated, but they will feel familiar: the tasks of 'business as usual', project management, resource allocation, all to deliver specified outcomes.

The *Exploration zone* is when things are more unfamiliar, for example when you're in times of significant change, when you're innovating, when you want different behaviours to get new outcomes. These times will all tend to have some elements of being 'beyond the known map'. In this type of activity your existing experience and expertise may or may not be quite so useful, and may at times even be a false friend.

We illustrate the Navigation and Exploration zones in this 'yin and yang' form because we like the complementary and flowing form of relationship that it suggests. Navigation and Exploration are not totally separate – this is not a polar relationship of opposites. Very often you'll face issues that lie more in one zone than the other, but most of our professional lives involve becoming adept and working with both, often at the same time.

How can understanding about Navigation and Exploration help disrupt organisations in positive ways?

EXPLORATION
Where existing expertise and experience can be a false friend
NAVIGATION
Where existing expertise and experience is a good enough guide

The first job of the framework is to acknowledge that the world isn't merely a technical problem for experts to fix. This is valuable because so much of our culture is about expertise and 'the right answer'. Simply knowing that it is legitimate to explore – that innovation can't happen without some elements of 'not knowing' – is extremely important in allowing new things to come about.

The second job is to help people spot when they are in one zone, when they're in the other, and when they're on the edge between them. Knowing where you are matters because you need to act differently in either case.

How do you know which zone you're in?

The main clue to spotting you're in the Navigation zone is very straightforward: it'll be familiar. The navigating world is one where your existing experience and expertise gives you a reliable sense of what is happening and what to expect.

You are likely to be entering the Exploration zone whenever people start talking about facing new problems: these can be genuinely totally new (such as the current virus), or new twists on familiar themes, such as entering new markets, finding new ways to achieve growth, creating a different way of connecting to customers and meeting their needs. What they have in common is that all of these demand that you develop fresh ways to see, act and organise to achieve a new way of working. In this zone, you are creating maps, not just following them.

What are the clues that tell you that the unknown is truly at hand?

Sometimes, of course, it is obvious. You are thrust into doing something that you haven't done before and consciously accept that you are stepping into unmapped space *for you*. The 'for you' is important, because someone somewhere may have done what you're doing, or someone in your team may have done it before. But the point is that you, in this organisation, with your products and customers, cultures and people, haven't done it. If you're smart you will spot that this is exploratory space and you and will deliberately step into it.

Sometimes it doesn't appear quite like that, and to some of the team (usually the top team) the path ahead seems innovative, but in an adjacent enough space to make them feel 'certain enough' that they can rest on existing skills and expertise. But you may notice some interesting phenomena, and if you do, it means that you have already moved into the Exploration zone without spotting it. For example...

- You may find yourself (if you're a member of the leadership team) wondering *why people aren't 'getting it'*? We often have top teams say to us, "We have a really clear strategy, why won't people buy in and step up?" If you are finding yourself frustrated by teams not buying in or stepping up, beware – you have crossed into the Exploration zone.
- You may be surprised that people have become *distracted*. They may be spending longer talking to each other at the water cooler or coffee machine. If you're really senior, you probably won't have noticed this, but you may hear evidence of it. It's hard for messages to reach the C-suite, and when they do

they're often edited and corrected. But if you get wind of this happening, be interested because it's a sign that you've left the known world and people are anxious.

- You may find that some of your teams seemingly '*disappear*' from view – it's really common at times like this for teams (or people) to get really busy on things. They might be too busy to work on your new ideas, because they've become overwhelmed by some aspects of their current workload. They've found a lot of fires that need immediate attention and this means that the new initiative isn't getting the traction you expected. This too is a sign that you've entered the Exploration zone.
- You might find teams *fighting* each other or *blaming* colleagues and suppliers. "We can't deliver what you're asking for, and it's not our fault, it's theirs…" or "We'd do this if only the leadership team understood xyz…"
- Finally, you might hear something like, "We can't do this right now, but we will be able to throw ourselves into making this happen when the new systems have been installed." Teams start waiting for some future event to release a blockage rather than working on the new frontier right now. This is a *false excuse* and a way of kicking the real work of exploring into the long grass.

If you continue to deploy solely the skills and

perspectives of past experience you will fail to reach the full potential of the situation, because you will never fully grasp the possibilities of exploration. You and your teams will be stuck in a world of incomplete maps. You may go on, even quite successfully at times, using the old maps and old expertise, never realising that a whole new world could have been yours if you had opened your eyes more fully to the new horizon.

Mastering exploration

It's extremely common when talking about strategy or change to use the metaphor of a journey with a destination: "We're here and we are headed for the sunlit uplands over there" (nobody ever heads for the drizzly lowlands). Our advice is to be very cautious about using 'destination' language at any time where you are uncertain and want others genuinely to join in exploring with you.

Think about explorers and expedition leaders of old. They had no maps, but were prepared for their process of exploration. They had the right team; they had the right equipment; they were fit. Focus on all these things in how you position the work to be done.

Those explorers also had one other important ingredient – a purpose. Notice that a purpose and a destination are different. Destination assumes you know the outcome, that you can describe the end point. Purpose doesn't do this. It says that the journey itself is important, that the reason for the exploration matters.

This is *not* a story of certainty. Perhaps another metaphor will help here – the knight on a white charger, who rides to the rescue heroically revealing a glorious plan. "Follow me, I've got the answer!"

We saw this at a business school, where a new CEO rode in with a clear plan. In the future the focus would solely be on large corporates, with the intention of maximising profit from each of them. Business development was no longer the responsibility of faculty but of large teams whose competencies included 'having the killer instinct'. The role of faculty was to turn up and teach people in their allotted programme. Staff were told: "This is what will make the business successful again". The story was clear, the boundaries extremely well defined. It was then simply a choice of whether to follow the knight or not.

By comparison, explorers invite people to join in the creation of the map, sharing with them the possibilities for the future. Explorers tell a story about their purpose and about the potential that lies over the horizon. The story invites others to come with them. Crafting and telling such a story is probably the most vital skill.

In tackling this invitation, there are five approaches that we have found to be extremely valuable. Here they are.

1. Start positive: take an 'appreciative' stance

Organisational life, and society in general, seems to have a huge appetite for looking at what's wrong, who failed and where the problem is. A lot of effort gets poured into deficit thinking, plugging the gap, fixing the problem. It's not obvious that this always works – after all, the railways still fail, the hospitals (even before the virus) still had waiting lists. So why not try a different starting point?

Start positive. Look for what is working and be curious about the energy and efforts that are making that happen. Explore what is positive and full of life, and you will tend to find more that is positive and full of life. Explore solutions, and you will tend to find more solutions. This is called taking an appreciative stance.

David Cooperrider and colleagues have been instrumental in creating a set of fundamental principles that lie behind such an approach. They can be summarised like this:

- *Words make worlds.* The reality we experience in companies, families, teams and other social organisations, is woven and constantly rewoven out of the conversations and other communications that happen (and don't happen) in them.
- *Inquiry isn't separate from change, it is part of change.* When we ask any question, we are participating in making the world. Asking safe and familiar questions helps the world to stay constructed 'as it is'. The moment people start raising a new question, the world is already starting to change.
- *What we pay attention to shapes things.* We have an infinite horizon of things we could focus on, so picking threads on which to focus our efforts really matters. We have a colleague who says "first steps can be fateful". This is why we *start* by taking an appreciative stance.

- *Work with hopeful images.* We all tend to be inspired to move towards the positive. Working with appreciative images of hope helps people to imagine more fully what such outcomes might be made of, and help them to see how they can use their skills and resources to bring this reality into being.
- *Positive intent builds energy and connection.* Establishing a positive image and starting some positive conversations is a sound way of inviting people to start working well together in support of something greater.

There are many ways of using this. One of the most popular is the Four-D approach. This involves organising projects around four groups of questions, all of them having an appreciative orientation. The four stages are:

- *Discover* – exploring what is already good, what's working, what resources you have
- *Dream* – imagining how it could be an even more brilliant outcome, organisation or strategy
- *Design* – creatively exploring how to work together to bring this about
- *Do* – sometimes also called Destiny or Deploy – working towards the aspiration that's been created.

We've known colleagues who create large scale projects of hundreds of people using this, and it is brilliant work. But you can equally bring this spirit to every small-scale action, each conversation, and have a big impact.

2. Invite and participate

If you explore alone, you won't have a rich enough set of experiences and perspectives to work from. Collective intelligence rules here!

The quality of participation is so important in good exploration, that we have developed our own framework that helps us ask good questions about whether we are getting really good participation and, if not, for helping to assess what might be getting in the way.

We call it the 5-P model. The Ps stand for Participation, Preferences, Power, Past patterns & Parental games. Let's explore each in turn and see its impact on inviting people to join in with this work.

Participation. In any organisational situation it is useful to notice who has been included in a given discussion or process and why, and, just as importantly, who has been excluded and why. Sometimes people are in, or out, as the result of physical constraints such as location and availability. But there may also be deeper and more personal reasons. People can be physically present but be excluded in the conversation, or can censor, silence or exclude themselves. Notice which voices are heard, and which are unheard, in this process and to what effect.

Preferences. On a very practical level, simple differences in personality preference can interfere with people's good intentions. In one situation, a CEO and a divisional head were both highly intuitive individuals, working on gut feel about the market and likely competitor response. The CFO was seen by them as a "details merchant", lacking in "big picture" ability. This was not overtly unfriendly, but the CFO was valued as a technical asset, whose doubts about the data behind the strategy being considered could not be heard because they were framed in 'fact seeking' rather than intuitive terms, and were thus dismissed as 'detail'.

Personality differences are common, and provided they are accepted, everyone can learn to respect others' ways of being and work with them. What obstructs good participation is not the difference in personality – difference is good – but the assumption that 'we' (in the above case, the CEO and the division head) are right and 'others' (the CFO) are seen as different and therefore wrong.

Power. Don't ignore power, uncomfortable though it is for many people to think about it. Here, we're thinking about it specifically in relation to participation in exploring. For example, how often have you been in an organisation, preparing a presentation, and been warned off making a particular point on the grounds that some senior manager 'doesn't want to hear that', or that it would be 'career limiting to tell her that'. Pay careful attention to the use of personal and political sources of power. Is it even acceptable to ask about power? Is a less loaded word like 'influence' used instead? Power affects what is said and what is unspeakable. It also affects who is listened to and who is ignored. Being able to bring this into conscious attention and to discuss the effect of its exclusion is important in bringing into the open and testing the mindsets in any exploring discussion.

Past patterns. We may be having our explorative conversation today, but the interaction is more complex than that. We are all also influenced by all the similar interactions we have ever had, from our earliest experiences in childhood through to similar conversations in our adult career. Particular individuals will often trigger reactions in us: people we respect and can do business with, or people we can scarcely credit as being worthy of the time of day. We are all aware of these reactions, but don't often stop to think how they affect serious business discussions. We should pay more attention to them because they can sometimes otherwise colour our responses in unintended ways.

The signs of past patterns interfering with today's conversation may be overt, but may also be very subtle – whose voice is heard, and who is never allowed into the real inner circle? When relationships appear too close or too broken to be explained rationally, maybe a past pattern is in play and is worth noticing.

"What might be happening to interfere in this relationship?" is often a good question to ponder at this point.

Parental games. We all fondly believe that in our organisational work we are rational adults talking with other rational adults. Sometimes the adult face slips and a more childlike kind of interaction occurs. When things get tough, or when people face extreme uncertainty, the child part of them often gets evoked. They look for someone – a leader, a government – to make it all safe for them. When leaders take clear, powerful, certain positions they tend to evoke the child response in others: that of asking the parent what to do. The child face can also be obstructive, spiteful, game-playing and keen on winning points.

It's important to be aware that this can happen in any organisational conversation, particularly when big power differences are involved. Participation depends on adults being in the room. Keep an eye open for child / parent games and intervene to change the situation. Encourage adult-to-adult conversations by asking open explorative questions, with the creation of a genuine sense of shared learning. By contrast, creating the sense that the 'leaders' know the answer but want us to give our input nonetheless, tends to reinforce child responses, which include the scepticism of the rebellious teenager.

3. Pay attention to the impact of your actions

As an explorer you are part of the bigger system, not just an objective observer. So you need to notice the effects that your actions are having on that system.

We have created a model that maps this onto a continuum.

Actions that support things as they are:

- Action with a "push" energy
- Telling and prescription
- Enforcement and compliance
- Logic and analysis above all
- Managing delivery of plans

Actions that support the search for new possibility in action:

- Action with a "pull" energy
- Invitation and allowing
- Curiosity, looking deeper
- Respect many kinds of data
- Emotional, embodied work is legitimate
- Working with energy flows

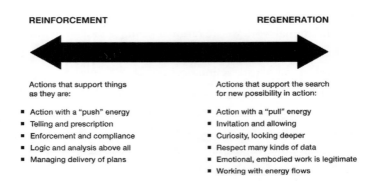

Reinforcement action. Activity coming from the left-hand side of this continuum comes from a place of knowing something. It is based on expertise and knowledge, and from having some kind of authority and power that comes from a role within that system.

From that position of certain knowledge, it can often be effective and appropriate to prescribe actions and deliver judgements based on expertise and experience. A doctor diagnosing appendicitis is coming from the legitimacy of knowing what these symptoms mean, and is trained to provide the solution. Similarly, in organisations, when the situation is familiar, using your expertise and authority to tell a clear and compelling story to spur people into action is exactly the right thing to do.

Even for the most enthusiastic disruptor, there will be lots of things that you don't need to challenge or change. The left side of the continuum is fine if you're turning the handle on what you do today.

Regenerative action. When you're really looking to disrupt thinking and action, reinforcement action isn't enough: you need to use the attributes and skills from the right-hand side of the continuum. Here the interventions are based on explicitly not knowing. This isn't a position of stupidity; it's a position of courage and authority, of clearly stating that this is a situation of not knowing so therefore good exploration is needed. Here the invitation comes with a 'pull' kind of energy. It has the spirit of invitation and openness about it.

Here it becomes especially important to state your assumptions and to be really interested in other people's assumptions too. This is an act of inviting curiosity about the deeper reasons for an action or a statement. Paying attention to these assumptions makes more of this usually hidden foundation visible. It invites others into an understanding, sharing and exploration of what is communicated.

4. Look wider, look deeper

Reinforcement action very often makes use of the prevailing logical language of organisations. It's the language of reports and emails, cold and analytical: you don't often find poems used to keep the business model exactly as it is. The language of emotion is largely avoided – excitement and energy are welcome in support of the status quo, but any darker or more difficult emotions are usually seen as a problem. It's often seen as safer to keep things logical. The messy business of being a human doesn't really get a full look in. Sometimes business is so cool and logical that it can feel like your work self is disembodied: a former client once said that her bosses just used their bodies to take their clever heads to meetings.

On the right-hand side of the continuum, where regenerative action happens, a richer set of data becomes legitimate. Things loosen up when you bring in more diverse ways of experiencing and exploring.

Expressive forms of art can provide new information: writing, story, poems, drawing and painting, sculpting, music making, movement, drama, clowning, improvisation and more. The wholly rational, linear, analytical language of business and organisation is simply insufficient to address the challenges we face as managers, leaders, as a society and as a species.

These richer ways of finding and acknowledging data are normally shunned, indeed suppressed, in organisational life. Richer and more diverse work gives us the opportunity to go beyond the common-space, brain-only workings of the organisational world. There is a depth and a freshness that comes from experiencing something deeply, in the senses and in the body, that feeds the potential for profound learning. Even more so if that experience is used to make visible the usually unstated assumptions and frames of the organisation, context or situation.

The more deeply people allow their richly sensed and embodied experience to inform their questioning of the given frame and to feed their creative re-framing of things, the bolder and more fruitful their work is likely to be.

Gestalt psychology asks everyone to 'lose their mind and come to their senses'. Stepping into the experience of being a living part of a messy creative planet is a vital part of this kind of work. Intellectualising before experiencing guarantees a separation from the living reality: disruptors need to step into action with all senses alert.

To allow sensory experience to do its work, it must be given time and space. Part of the work of looking wider and deeper is to create experiences and exercises that temporarily derail the ever-present 'brainy' mode of organisation and leadership. This is essential to stopping the rush from experience directly into expertise and problem-solving based on old frames and existing ways of seeing. Suspending judgement is a crucial stage in learning to truly appreciate what is going on, before you leap in to fix it.

5. Expect the unexpected and keep learning

How many times in your organisational life have you seen a PowerPoint showing a circle (normally somewhere on the left hand side of the page) indicating where you (the organisation) are now and a straight line pointing to another circle on the right, indicating an end point at some future time horizon? If your experience is anything like ours, we're sure your answer will be 'often'.

There is nothing wrong at all with developing this kind of strategic intent: 'This is where we are now and this is the story – in more detail or less – of what we plan to do to get to a particular end point'. It can be good to have a compelling, differentiated, well thought through, rigorously grounded story that can be used to explain things to your teams, your funders, and any other stakeholders. But don't go away with the idea that this intent is the same as what the actual outcome will be. As the old military adage has it, 'No plan survives contact with the enemy'.

The straight line will almost undoubtedly take a very different trajectory, and will probably lead to a circle (or a square or a triangle or a strange new blob-like shape) in a different place. This is much more how things actually unfold – more like a dance, hopefully an alert and intelligent one, between intent and an unfolding, complex, responsive and unpredictable reality.

Some colleagues of ours long ago developed a model that captures this. We have continued to develop and refine it over the years. We think of it as the 'messy reality' model. We find it hugely valuable in our work. Many organisations get 'aha' moments from working with it.

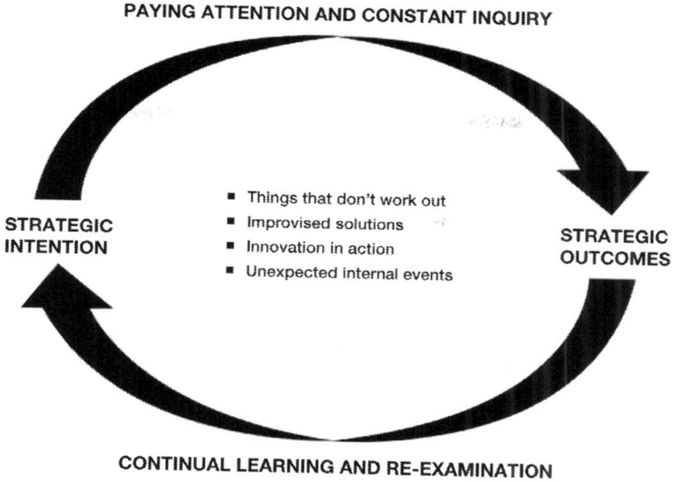

The messy reality model reminds us that developing and implementing strategic ideas is not just a cool rational act. The development of 'intent' is itself loaded with all of the politics, power and psychology that go on in groups. Developing a good strategic intention comes from getting the right balance between analytical work, creative input and the testing (and retesting) of assumptions to offset stuck thinking, narrow ideas and Groupthink. "We can't see the whole picture, but we can see more of the picture if we collaborate intelligently." Continually ask, as you make strategic intentions: how good is the data on which you are deciding? How can everyone be sure of what they are seeing? What are we all assuming that might be limiting or dangerous? How can we all be aware of the biases in our decision making that might trip us up?

Once you have your intent – perhaps beautifully captured in your slide pack – you go out into the world with it as your plan, knowing that all kinds of things will happen that were never in it.

First, people are people, and it won't be implemented as you expect. Some of the intent just won't work. Competitors do something you didn't expect. Customers don't like an idea. The technology doesn't light up. Your staff just won't do it like you planned they would. All manner of other things get in the way and cause the intent to falter.

All this is normal, inevitable even. The question is: 'Is your organisation able to talk openly about things that aren't working out, or is bad news hidden under the carpet?' Unless you cultivate a culture in which it is legitimate to notice difficulties, problems and unexpected adverse news, and to express doubts about the way things are going, you won't spot the difficulty at an early stage. The sooner you spot the signs of failure, the sooner you can learn, act, adjust and refocus. Jack Welch once said, "If you're not failing, you're not trying hard enough." What he meant was fail fast, small and cheaply. Be alert to signs of trouble and learn from them quickly. That's smart. Pretending all is well when it isn't: that's dumb.

Second, your people will improvise and adapt along the way. They will just invent stuff, solve problems, subvert systems and processes and help customers in ways you never expected. This is strategy in action. The question is whether you spot it, understand it, nurture what is good and useful and embrace it… or whether you kill it off and fire the maverick improvisers.

It's so easy to say to the last words above, "Oh, I'd never do that." But when it's your pet strategy that's being subverted, your brand focus that's being challenged… What do you actually do, at appraisal time, when considering promotions, when giving rewards? Who do you favour: the compliant or the responsive? Every gesture you make makes the culture. The more you build a culture where you learn about staff taking steps that are strategy in action, the more you learn about what experiments are actually going on and what is coming out of them.

Third, stuff happens. Events you never expected will come about and you will respond to them. There are lots of threats and opportunities that just crop up and demand you do something. How quickly does news of these flow to you from the staff most able to see and feel it? How do you promote the culture and practices by which everyone is aware of what counts as strategic news? How do you have processes that make it easy to get this news to the right people and into the strategic thinking of the organisation?

In this framework, the organisation works at best like a nervous system, constantly sensing and testing the environment for small signals about what is working and what isn't, constantly evaluating the experiment that is at the heart of all strategic action. This is a much more powerful way of working with strategy – a wider and richer view than the commonplace 'plan and deliver' model. Using a richer way of thinking about strategy is truly an act of revolution in itself.

A disciplined approach to bring it all together

All the above material comes from a technique known as Action Inquiry. In our experience it is the most powerful way to harness passion and action in a rigorous process to get new ideas into practice and deliver results.

The world is complex and made up of assumptions and stories. To be effective in this complexity and construction, you need to take a systemic view, seeing the world as a pattern where actions and reactions are connected but not necessarily in predictable ways. There is much that cannot be known and much that cannot be seen, so collaborative working and diversity becomes essential, as they allow you to see more, know more and explore more. Others can see things that you cannot.

Action Inquiry can develop a community of people with the skills to advance this kind of practice, day in and day out, and in doing so change the world in which we live. It goes on at several levels, usually at the same time:

Individual inquiry is the root of all good Exploration work. It is about being rigorously curious about yourself, your actions, your intent, your reasoning, your theoretical groundings, your perceptions, biases, your emotions and your bodily reaction to things.

Participative inquiry involves exploring *with others* something of interest to everyone involved. We're seeing this right now at the height of the pandemic crisis, as the medical teams we're working with collaborate in new ways to experiment and learn about how to reconfigure and improvise to respond to shifting needs.

Participative inquiry can range from work with groups of colleagues to large, formally contracted projects. At the heart of the work is always a group of people who have agreed to come together to explore an issue of mutual concern.

Using these methods, you may not necessarily find a 'right' answer straight away. This work often takes several rounds of trying things, learning, trying something else and changing tack. The world can call on us to have more than one bite at something – and if the something is important enough to us, most of us are willing to stick to it for a while, trying new things.

This allows for *cycles of activity and learning* to take place. Each one involves:

- planning to do something
- preparing how to do something
- inviting the right people to do it
- taking the action
- noticing what happens
- reflecting on what happened, both the expected and the unexpected
- making sense of the outcomes, perhaps by going back to some relevant ideas, theories, perspectives
- coming up with a next action to take the work forward another step.

All of this together is a cycle of inquiry, a complete round of action, investigation, sense-making and a resulting new action. We have a mnemonic to help you remember the stages of this cycle. It's called SOARING, which is what we hope Action Inquiry will help you and your organisation do.

- **S** **Start where you are**. Wherever you are right now, that is the place to begin.
- **O** **Observe**. What's going on? Look for the data: patterns; what's going well; anomalies; difficulties.
- **A** **Act**. Take action and notice actions (including no action and reluctance or compulsion to act.)
- **R** **Reflect, review, refine**. What's the consequence of your action? Is this serving your purpose? To what extent are the outcomes useful and good? What might shift it for the better?
- **I** **Investigate, inquire, imagine**. Dig in, see what else is possible. How else could you look at this? What other possible actions could arise from seeing it differently, from poking the system in a fresh way?
- **N** **New action**. What new experiment or fresh action draws you? What step will you take?
- **G** **Go around again**. This work moves in cycles of action and inquiry, broadening, shifting and deepening to move the work forward.

All the time you'll be looking at both your individual inquiry and the shared inquiry. At an individual level you will be asking, 'What was my part in it and why did it go as it did? How else might I do this to get great outcomes?' At the shared level, ask, 'What are we learning together about creating the future difference we are trying to bring about?'

Each time you do a cycle, it provides the inspiration and insight for the next cycle. Over time, therefore, these cycles of inquiry build on each other to become wider and deeper. Future cycles can be created to answer questions raised in earlier cycles, or to amplify things that went well to get more of that outcome, or to try different things in an area when the outcome wasn't so good.

After a while you'll notice that this becomes a way of being. You can plan formal cycles of inquiry – as you will if you're doing a big shared change inquiry. But you'll also find that cycles crop up 'for free': every conversation, every time you read a book or an article, or get an idea from a blog on the web, or take a reflective stroll. Every one of these is also an action with consequences that becomes part of your practice of inquiry.

So how do you do Action Inquiry, step-by-step? Here are some ways forward that work:

- Really turn up
- Listen
- Make notes & use them
- Be curious about the big picture
- Take a systemic view

Really turn up

How many times do we *really* attend to what is actually going on? To what extent do we just go to the places we usually go and see only the things we usually see, because that's what we are expecting?

Think of some of the meetings you go to, especially the regular ones. Do people keep doing and saying the same things? So many meetings involve the presentation of pre-prepared material. They are people presenting what they always do, in order to make the argument they always make to people who are not really listening because they're hearing what they expect to hear. We call these 'frozen chicken' meetings. Everything involves the exchange of pre-packed, deep frozen positions. Nothing really gets thawed out or tasted. In our experience, quite a lot of organisational life takes this form.

There's an act of will involved in deciding to really turn up somewhere properly, rather than 'turning up and doing the minimum'. It starts with you deciding that you are going to experience some parts of your life differently. Then you allocate time and energy to paying attention more fully in the situations you've chosen.

Start small. Pick one meeting, or even one conversation within a meeting, and decide to really notice what happens in it as if everything in it were new to you.

- Set aside a few minutes before you go into the meeting room. Just sit and gather your attention.
- If your mind is very busy from the last thing you've

done, take a moment to make a mental (or actual) note of what it is busy with, then make a conscious decision to 'park' this business for later.

- Notice how you are feeling. Are the feelings attached to the last meeting, to the one you're now going to, or to something else? No need to try to change any of this – just notice what you're feeling and what it's about.
- Spend one minute taking a few slower deeper breaths and noticing the calming effect on your body and your mind.
- Finally, focus on going into the meeting with the intention of really turning up and being 100% there.

When you really pay attention in this way it can be a bit like arriving in a strange town, with new sounds and smells, with an unfamiliar street layout. You have to pay attention to everything in this new place; nothing can be assumed.

Listen

What do you do, once you are in this meeting (or whatever event you have chosen to attend in your new, fully alert, positive disruptor mode)?

You listen. We use this word in its widest sense of paying deep attention, in other words listening to the sounds but also observing behaviour and thinking about the implications of all you perceive.

Listen for the *explicit content*. This is the more obvious

content of the conversation. Someone is telling you about something. What are the facts?

Listen for the *emotional undercurrent*. Every conversation has at least one of these. It might be measured and neutral; the conversation might be about some really straightforward stuff, at least on the surface. But if you listen fully you might notice that a lot of how the person who is speaking is actually feeling is not expressed in the explicit flow of words. Sometimes this can be easy to spot. If someone is obviously really angry or excited, their body language, tone of voice and the nature of the words they choose will give this away. But often we don't get such obvious signals. Someone could be very angry, upset or hopeful, but they are looking perfectly 'normal' to us.

This is where we need to listen out for the subtler cues they might be giving us in the words they choose and the very subtle body language signs. Look out for things like:

- How are they sitting? Is there anything in their stance that seems at odds with the words coming from their mouth?
- What do their facial expressions tell you?
- How would you judge their voice in comparison to what it normally is?
- What emotion-based words are they using?

You might notice that the facts and the emotions don't match. Sometimes someone is telling you about the exciting new plan for their department, but somehow the tone of voice or the way they are sitting tells another story. Learn to become very interested in times where the body, story, emotions and energy seem out of line with each other.

Be interested in the speaker's *intent and assumptions.* Think about why you are being told this particular material at this particular time. Notice what the speaker seems inclined to do about the situation they're describing. This is probably the hardest of all the ways of listening.

You are not out to second-guess the speaker's intention, but to learn more. You can always check out your observation with a question to see if you're hearing things that aren't there. What you are trying to do is really understand why the person is telling you about this thing, in this way, right now. Basically, you're being really interested in them and their story. Doing this is giving someone the gift of your attention.

As you listen you'll begin to notice *the impact of what is being said on you.* Over time, you will see how you are drawn to some stories more than to others, more to some kinds of speaker than to others. As you practice listening, notice your own patterns, get to know your biases, so you don't mix up your own emotions with someone else's.

Pay particularly close attention to *language choices and usage.* The kind of words a person uses, the imagery buried in the words – these are all full of data about how the person's world is made up. Quite often problems arise because everybody in the room is using a different mental map, each of which is full of different images and metaphors. There is a 'stuckness' that stays around, simply because no-one has noticed its roots in language. If you're in a change meeting and mentally preparing for battle while someone else is getting ready to embark on a journey of discovery, then it's very likely that your conversations will constantly be at odds with each other.

Make notes and use them

During his famous voyage on HMS *Beagle*, Charles Darwin used a series of 'field notebooks' to record his observations. These were identified by letter – Notebook A, Notebook B and so on. Each covered a specific set of experiences, such as his visit to Galapagos or his time in Sydney. He knew that if he didn't write down what he saw as soon as he could, his memory would muddle things. Experiences, new connections, speculations: all were recorded. This is the model we suggest for anyone involved in positive disrupting.

The great advantage you have over Darwin is that you can keep records in any form that suits you. No need to use actual notebooks, although many people still find that that is their preferred method. It's absolutely fine to use your phone or tablet if that's what you prefer. If your way of working is more visual, use it. Scrapbooks, artists' journals, an annotated photo library – whatever works best for you.

Record as much as you can. Go to a meeting; write down what happened. Anxious about something? Jot yourself a note to help you recall the context and the feelings later on. If something goes exactly to plan, record it. If something goes unexpectedly well, write it down. If nothing happened at all, don't lose sight of that, either.

Don't feel this is self-indulgent. It is work to make you more effective and of greater service to others.

You will look back on these notebooks, journals or photo records weeks and months later and suddenly you'll start to see a movement or a pattern that would get utterly overlooked if you were to rely on memory alone. Memory is always re-creating and re-editing to fit current experience. By tracking what happens as it happens, including the movements in your attention, perception and insights, you'll see more of how your inner and outer work is progressing, and understand much more about your interaction with the obstacles you are encountering (both inner and outer).

The following prompts may be helpful in getting you started:

- *Where* are you? What's the context of what you're doing (of this meeting, this conversation).
- *What* is happening there?
- *When*? Date your notes and notice where in the flow of a process you are.
- *Who* is involved in this? Who isn't?
- *Why*? Become very interested in why this thing is happening now. Why did this meeting seem to be the right (or the wrong) meeting at this time? Why did this meeting (right or not) happen now? Why did this agenda, and not that one, come about? Why did these people and not those people, these ways of looking not those ways of looking, get selected?
- *How* did you go about being involved? How did you prepare? How did you turn up? How did it go? How can you make sense of it? How can you

do something different next time as a result of the experience you just had?

Having made these notes, use them. Reflect on them right away. Reflect a little later. Reflect again a lot later. Write down what you notice when you do this reflection.

An interesting exercise is to experience your notes (in whatever form you have made them) as if they were written by someone else. Become really interested in this strange, new person. Ask yourself some questions such as:

- What is it they are experiencing?
- What assumptions are they making?
- What are the consequences of their assumptions?
- What language and imagery do they use?
- Do they seem to keep coming back to something? A pattern, a common way of thinking, some questions that won't go away?
- How is their work going? How are they reacting to it?
- If you were to give them some advice about their next step or steps, what would it be?

Be curious about the big picture

Our observations about making notes are quite detailed – as they are meant to be. Most disciplines are built on the back of the mastery of small skills. But positive disruptors are also relentlessly curious about the 'bigger' aspects of organisational life, and always looking for clues that will give them insight into this. Think of the material in the book so far and look out for…

- *Identity.* How does the group – the team, the organisation – make its identity by what it does do and what it doesn't do, by what it is like to be in the group and by what is not acceptable?
- *Patterns and ritual dances.* What are the routines? Maybe there isn't actually a company song(!) but there will be something that does a similar job. Some of the rituals will be about maintaining identity and culture; others will show what's important and the focus of attention. Noticing how people feel about the patterns and rituals will also be informative. Do people long for the annual round of evaluations and performance bonuses? What about the team events? What do the stories you hear tell you?
- *Participation.* Start to notice who's 'in' and who's not, and why. Who controls inclusion and exclusion? What is it cool to be part of and what is uncool but vital? Who gets listened to and who can't get heard?
- *Power.* What sorts of power do you see and how does the power come about? Who sets the agenda? Who decides what issues are considered to go on the agenda? How do people react to the notion that power exists? Why? What is your reaction to the power processes you see?

- *Unwritten rules*. What does everybody know that isn't written down? What can get you fired? How are heroes made? What gets you into the newsletter? Is it the same thing that gets you paid more and promoted higher? What would never get spoken about but should be?
- *Sacred cows*. What beliefs, products, processes and people are beyond critique? What is untouchable or unsayable? What is taboo, so much so that you'd feel guilty even thinking about it?
- *Language and imagery*. How do things get described? Are we a super-tanker trying to become a speedboat? Are we putting more effort into the engine room, or cutting out the dead wood? How's it going in our must-win battles?
- *Formal and informal*. Every organisation has its formal systems (the structure, processes and procedures, systems, the calendar of events) and its informal ways of working (do decisions get made in the meeting room, or outside where the smokers congregate, as happened at one organisation we know?). How much effort goes into each? Where is the real work done? Does power work the same way in both? Are they equally important?

This seems a big ask, so don't rush it. Just be curious in your own mind about these things, and see what you start noticing.

Take a systemic view

We spend our lives in systems, so it's odd that so much of our education and training prepares us for a life of seeing things as separate parts. Learning to see more of the system is partly about unlearning this.

When you see the system, you explain things at the level of interconnections and interdependencies rather than the units they're made of. You start to see ways of acting that make sense in a sub-system, but which make no sense at all in a higher-level system of which the sub-system is just a part.

Failing to put things in a bigger context can lead to the phenomenon of the 'perverse incentive'. A call centre was told that it had to reduce the length of time clients were kept waiting for the phone to be answered. No other instructions were given. So it cut down the number of phones. This meant that no phone went unanswered for long, but many callers got engaged signals.

Someone taking a systems view might ask why so many customers needed to call in the first place. What problems were they calling about? Could the problems be resolved so that the calls were no longer necessary?

One of the main things to notice about systems is that you are usually (or even always) in the system as a participant and not standing apart as some kind of external observer. When you talk about the health system or the financial system, it is not an 'it' somehow apart from yourself, but a nest of interactions in which you are deeply involved.

Once you realise you are not a solely rational, impartial,

detached being, but an intricately complicit maker of and participant in the systems that you are seeking to change, you understand the importance of the disciplined nature of the positive disrupting approach, particularly the attention you need to pay to your personal role and attachments.

One of the pioneering and most influential thinkers in the field of systems was Gregory Bateson. He was ruthless in exposing the arbitrary boundaries that humans often make between themselves and the rest of the living world. His *Steps to an Ecology of Mind* has proved one of the most influential books of all time in this field (though it is not an easy read).

He saw the individual 'mind' as part of a larger cognitive process that defined human cognition, which he called 'Mind'. The human fantasy of separateness from other aspects of the living world was to him a flawed boundary definition. His book was published in 1972, just before the energy crises of 1973-79. His analysis of the flaws in reductionist thinking (having too small a view of a system and ascribing to yourself a special and independently superior place with respect to it) proved prophetic.

It's simply not possible for humans to see the whole of a system, but we can do our best not to be blinded by bias or inertia into taking a view that's too small. Seeing richer and seeing more is always possible.

Anyone serious about positive disrupting will need to pay attention as far as possible to systems and connected processes. The more you work to improve your awareness of these and how they work, the finer your awareness becomes and the more you become able to intervene.

A matter of time

So, you think all the above sounds potentially really useful. But a question will soon arise. "How on earth can I expect to fit that into my already packed diary? And that's assuming that I remember to do it at all. I love the ideas but it's just too much to do, another thing to think of."

Stop! All the techniques we suggest are small. Maybe begin by practicing them in one meeting a week, nothing more. Making sure you're really present before the meeting starts takes 2 or 3 minutes. Capturing notes and images during the meeting, and reflecting afterwards can begin with a 5 minute self-review of what was happening, with perhaps another 5 minutes at the end of the day, and perhaps a slightly longer time (15 mins or so) at a later date.

Using the downtime of any commute can be a great place to practice your self-reflection, as it's stealing back time that would likely otherwise be wasted. Alternatively, practice the discipline of getting out of bed 5 minutes earlier than usual and think about the day ahead over a calming cup of tea.

You can get help to do this. In one organisation, a relatively senior leader – let's call her Katie – asked a peer to help her become more reflective. They spent several hours a week together in a large leadership team meeting that could, at times, become quite challenging. Katie knew that she was prone to losing her temper when her frustration became too much for her. So, for a few weeks, straight after the end of each meeting, Katie and her colleague would huddle together for a few minutes and Katie would get feedback about how she had come across in the meeting, what had worked well and what hadn't. Over time, as Katie became more skilled at moderating her own behaviour within the meeting, the need for these huddles diminished.

It's not about spending lots of time; it's about spending small bits of time effectively.

That doesn't answer the question about how you remember to do it. That varies according to preferences. One leader we know used his calendar to prompt him. Someone else used the anticipated presence of a particular colleague in a meeting as a prompt to make her really pay attention and be present.

Once you've decided to give it a go then do so. There's a reason that we've called the different techniques and methods 'practices'. They need to be practiced. Remember doing piano or violin scales when you were younger? Chances are you were told that 5 minutes practice every day was better than 30 minutes once a week. The same applies to the practices of disrupting.

Sustaining yourself in the work

You're going to have to invest a lot of time in thinking about yourself and your personal change. This approach to personal change isn't self-indulgence; it's rigorous. You are woven into everything around you, part of the problem, caring about the change, actively working towards something better, so you need to pay a lot of attention to yourself.

Look hard at how you are. Study your biases, attitudes,

ways of connecting – warts and all. Get the help of critical friends to challenge you.

If you do this inner work well, it becomes the ongoing basis of all you do. It is never finished, either. If you stop being rigorously self-assessing, you stop being able to pursue disruption with real quality. Meister Eckhart, the 13th century theologian, philosopher and mystic, said, "The outer work will never be puny if the inner work is great." If you do weak inner work, don't expect great outcomes in your efforts. Inner work matters.

So, we invite you to go to the lighthouse. This is a device we have been using for some years and it serves well as a focus of reflective practice, a way of looking deeper.

Imagine a lighthouse, a tall, strong structure rising from deep foundations embedded into hard rock, built to withstand gale-force winds and the power of the sea. At its top, a bright beam shines out, warning ships of the presence of that rock.

Think of yourself as this lighthouse. Describe your formal roles: role and title in the organisation, number of direct reports, size of budget, geographical responsibility, any other material descriptions of your formal leadership position. If you do not yet have such a position remember that, once you decide to promote positive disruption, you will still be leading informally. Think of the people you influence, challenge and inspire.

Next, think about the light that shines from the lighthouse and reflect on the nature and quality of your leadership light. How would you describe yourself? How would others describe you? Use the following questions but do not feel limited to these issues: all self-description is good.

- What sort of energy do you see in yourself / do others see in you?
- What emotions do you most associate with yourself / what emotions might others associate with you?
- What sort of decision maker are you? How would others describe your decision making?
- How do you organise yourself and your team? What do others experience?
- What other facets of yourself feature in the 'light' that people experience from you?

Which of the characteristics you've written (you may have several for each of these questions) do you believe burn brightest? These are the ones that everyone in touch with you would agree are your best aspects.

What is the downside of these brilliant bright aspects of you? Bright lights also cast shadows. What shadows does your light cast for you and for others?

Now take your self-reflections to a critical friend. Perhaps they've done the same exercise themselves. In which case, probe and challenge each other. Act as coaches. Help each other deepen the self-reflection.

Use this process well and reflect on it often and deeply. The insights can be profound and will be an important part of continuing to build and nourish quality in your work.

3 THE INNER OBSTACLES

Let's begin with an old model. Back in 1943, psychologist Abraham Maslow proposed a theory of individual motivation. He said that all humans have a number of inbuilt needs and that these are organised in a specific order. He also said that one set of needs has to be met before the next can be addressed.

Maslow's so-called 'hierarchy of needs' has almost become pop-psychology these days. It has been criticised for lack of robust testing. Maybe – but it remains a very useful reminder that we all have a range of needs that drive our behaviour, and that they often express themselves without us noticing.

- At the most basic level people have *physical* needs. Without air, water and food none of us will survive.
- Next up is *security*. People need to have shelter and safety, a stable harbour from the storms.

- Then come social needs (Maslow called these our needs for 'belongingness and love'). As a species we like to belong: to groups, families, tribes, communities and organisations. Most people expend a lot of energy in meeting these needs.
- Higher up are *esteem* needs. This term covers both the need for self-esteem and the respect of others. The desires for status, prestige and power are part of this.
- At the pinnacle of the triangle sit the so-called *self-actualisation* needs: the spiritual quests, creative activity, seeking and finding our authentic flourishing self.

You might ask what this has got to do with obstacles to change. The answer is 'a lot'.

The group that we belong to is often seen as operating at level three in the hierarchy, but it is more. It is a way of meeting basic needs. Most of us have worked hard to belong to some organisation or other, not just to belong but to put food on the table, pay the mortgage, look after our dependents, get health cover and a pension for our old age.

It can be a way of meeting higher needs, too. Lucky individuals are also part of organisations where esteem needs are met, where they gain recognition and prestige. Really lucky individuals find slots where their work allows them to meet the highest level of needs, to live out some aspects of what they believe is their deep purpose, in service of others, through creativity or spiritual goals. In these situations, work can become what Khalil Gibran called 'love made visible'.

These benefits mean that people will resist change for reasons at every level of the hierarchy. People will go along with a lot to remain safe, to hold onto the salary and the pension. As the Pulitzer Prize winning writer Upton Sinclair once said, "It is difficult to get a man to understand something when his salary depends on his not understanding it."

People will willingly accept the norms and habits of workplaces and other groups because, when they don't, they become excluded, losing group membership and identity. For some people, their very self-actualization depends on playing by the organisation's rules and acting out roles in the organisation's stories.

A world made of stories

Making and sharing stories is how people build relationships and bring groups, communities and organisations together. You are part of an organisation because you accept and share its story and see yourself in it.

But supposing the story becomes the only one that can be told?

The power of story is well illustrated by Enron, a highly regarded US company back in the 1990s. It was driven by stories. Stories of being the bold mavericks who re-wrote the rules of the US energy market. Stories about being 'the smartest guys in the room'. The stories spread beyond the company: investors bought into them, the media bought into them. Regulators even bought into them: Enron persuaded financial regulators to accept new ways of measuring profit.

Stories can, as the ultimate Enron story reminds us, be dangerous illusions. It filed for bankruptcy in November 2001, and dragged its auditors down with it.

All organisations are made up of stories, and a large part of the value inherent in any business consists of the story it tells. When the stock market 'values' a company, it is mostly about investors putting a cash value on their belief in a story. The investors are saying that they believe that this organisation has a strategy they think will live into the future and that this management team can deliver that story. When the story stops being credible, the value collapses.

Stories can be contagious. They are, as novelist Patrick Naess wrote, 'wild creatures'. They can run loose and bring about consequences that no one sees coming. No one in Enron was stupid, certainly not the top management team. But we doubt very much that, when they made heroes out of the company's maverick innovators and market opportunists, Enron's senior leaders realised the full implication for the organisation of the stories they were celebrating.

In some ways the story of Enron is a tragedy. A brilliant company undone by being bewitched by its own story. Part of the story was that this was a company so cool, so smart, that the normal rules weren't made for it, and that the organisation could and deserved to rewrite the way the game was played. Up to a point this was successful. Enron did play a part in reshaping the energy industry around the world. But they believed that their story went wider, and that they were the genius company that could reshape everything, that all markets for anything could also be fair game for Enron. There was little room for humility in this story. In flying too close to the sun, the company suffered the fate of Icarus.

Even brilliantly successful stories need to be challenged and changed – and if change is impossible, if challenge is seen as treachery, then the organisation is on the road to ruin. As writer Salman Rushdie once wisely noted, "If you can't reinvent your story when times change, you are powerless."

Tricks of the mind

We all make sense of the world through the biological system of our senses and nervous system. These play some really interesting games that can affect what we see and what we ignore. The next section is a quick guide to three aspects of cognitive psychology that play a role in making people blind to the need for change. These are: spotlight attention, perception and processing, and confirmation bias.

Spotlight attention – we just don't see all of it!

There's infinitely more happening in the world than any one individual can pay attention to. We all have incredibly selective attention, and it saves us from going completely crazy because of the sheer amount of data out there. We just don't see most of what is going on.

Stage magic plays on this fact. The illusionist directs the audience's attention to something and, while their focus is there, the trick is performed and they don't notice the sleight of hand.

This was brilliantly illustrated by The Invisible Gorilla Study by Daniel Simons and Christopher Chabris in 1999. Participants were asked to watch a video clip of basketball and count passes between white shirted players and to ignore passes between their dark shirted opponents. In the middle of the clip a human in a full gorilla suit strode into the game and beat its chest before exiting stage left. Almost no-one spotted it.

Psychologist Richard Wiseman does the same in his widely viewed Quirkology videos (www.quirkology.com), most notably The Amazing Colour Changing Card Trick.

Both are beautiful examples of 'spotlight attention': focus here, miss events there.

Corporate life is crammed full of focus-grabbers like these – KPIs and business plans for example – that are easily mistaken for the whole of 'reality'. Once people focus solely on 'their' numbers they tend to become blind to things that are not being measured, even if those things are massively important. The measurement indicators become the story and the changing world becomes invisible, or an inconvenient truth that cannot be spoken about because the performance metrics have come to be seen as all that matters.

Perception and processing – it's patterns all the way

There's another part of our psychology that gets mixed up in limiting our ways of seeing. Humans love patterns and we tend to find ones that are familiar to us.

In the 1950s, psychologist Karl Dallenbach was trying to understand how it is we recognise things when we see them. Why, he wondered, don't we have to go through a prolonged analytical process to work out what we're looking at – instead we just seem to know what things are? For example, once you learn what a cow is, you don't spend a lot of time deliberately recognising (or acknowledging that you've recognised) cows every time you see one; you just know that you've seen one.

The answer turns out to be because we automatically organise our perceptions in 'clusters' – baskets of stuff that's familiar enough to make sense. Our brains process data 'top-down'. Our neural system doesn't just receive data 'bottom-up', neutrally, from the world. It processes it to make sense of what's there by seeking to fit the raw data to known patterns.

There are lots of examples of ambiguous images – such as the face of Jesus popping up in a snowdrift – to show that we humans have a huge (and sometimes unhelpful) talent for finding patterns that make sense to us. That's how these images work: once someone sees the familiar 'figure' in the chaotic background of data, others will see it too. Once it is seen, it becomes very difficult indeed to unsee it.

A wonderful example is that of songs played backwards, which sound like nonsense until someone gives you a set of lyrics that somehow 'fits' a pattern in the noise. Then all you can hear is that 'lyric'. That's why some people claim that Led Zeppelin's *Stairway to Heaven* contains satanic messages when you play it backwards. UK comedian Peter Kay has created a brilliant comic set using exactly this effect, providing hysterical alternative lyrics to extracts from famous pop songs.

And, of course, this doesn't happen just with snowdrifts, Led Zeppelin (backwards) and Peter Kay, it happens in every meeting you ever go to, on every sales trip you attend. You don't see the world as it is, and you don't hear exactly what's going on. Instead you see and hear what you have filters and maps of reality that are sufficient for you to see and hear. Generally what lies outside those runs the risk of getting filtered out as noise. This is what makes strategic horizon scanning a bit tricky. If you're not expecting it, or if you are actively looking for something else, you have very little chance of actually spotting and understanding genuinely new stuff.

Confirmation bias – accepting what we expect

The brain's wiring is primed towards the familiar, and this helps to create and maintain those familiar patterns. Everywhere you turn you find evidence that confirms and re-confirms your ways of seeing because that's what you are looking for.

This is the well-known phenomenon of confirmation bias, which is the frequently occurring tendency for people to see evidence that supports their position and to discount any facts or observations that run in another direction.

Scientific researchers are taught to watch out for this. If they are testing a hypothesis, they are told to guard against any tendency to seek confirmation and instead to try to find ways to knock their own ideas down. Science works by trying to prove an idea is wrong and only accepting it as 'good enough for now' if it can't be rejected. It must be rare indeed for any of us to bring such rigour to our everyday lives –

but it could serve us very well to be a bit more scientific in checking out our biases in leadership and in organisational life.

From the Enron story to the polarisations in society that have led to populist politics, it is clear that confirmation bias is a strong force. The 'bubble effect' of social media exacerbates this, since it is very easy for people only to subscribe to the information they want to see, and for any contradictory information to be rejected right away as 'fake news'.

We all play our part in letting obstacles to change develop consciously because to do so enables us to satisfy some really deep needs, to be safe, to belong, to be powerful. We do so unconsciously because our perceptual processes are 'wired in' and our language comes to us as a given.

These aspects of individual psychology are part of the story. There is another thread, when we turn to placing our personal stories within the shared story of groups.

Groups cause problems

They say it takes a village to raise a child. This section will focus on three aspects of group psychology:

- Hierarchy and power
- In-groups and out-groups
- Behaviour when times get tough.

Hierarchy and power

Aristotle was spot on when he said, "Man is a political animal." Give any group of people limited resources and a decision to make, and you'll see politics and power emerge. We have been involved in experiments in 'flat', non-hierarchical working. Many people have a fantasy that such super-agile structures will be free of political hierarchy. They're not. Instead, they can be brutal.

In every group of humans there will be a power structure and a formal, or informal, hierarchy. This power structure, and the patronage that often goes with it, acts to super-charge all of the factors already discussed, as resources are allocated and withheld and tasks and rewards assigned. When a story or a frame has the backing of a powerful leader or leadership group it can become even more deeply entrenched.

In-groups and out-groups

A fascinating social psychology experiment from the 1970s showed that very little difference is needed for the members of one group to start discriminating against members of another.

Henri Tajfel and his colleagues got together 48 teenage boys and showed them pictures by two artists, Kandinsky and Klee (the subjects had never heard of either). The boys were then asked to express views on the paintings, after which they were divided into two groups, the Klee group and the Kandinsky group. This being a psychological experiment, there was a trick – the actual criterion for dividing them up was totally random, but the boys thought they had in some way selected themselves for group membership by the views they expressed on the paintings. The boys were given tasks to do, then asked to evaluate others' performance. Guess what: the Kandinskys gave better marks to other Kandinskys, and the Klees gave better marks to the Klees.

Now just imagine that membership of groups isn't arbitrary. You're in a large organisation and the in-group adheres to the powerful leader and the 'legitimate' story. The other group challenges the story and offers other ways of seeing the world. Add into this the power dynamic of the hierarchical leader backing the in-group with resources and patronage, and you have a recipe for silencing and exclusion.

We have seen this happen again and again in organisational life, where a dissident faction with strategically useful but organisationally inconvenient data is shut out, isolated and undermined. Power determines what counts as truth; the accepted truth then drives behaviour, and the opportunity for difference is eradicated.

This happens all of the time, even when groups and organisations are working well. But it can get even more powerful when times get tough.

Group behaviour under stress

Wilfred Bion studied groups most of his life. He noticed that generally groups work quite well when the task of the group is clear and when roles within the group are settled. He also noticed that when groups hit turbulent times, things got more 'primitive'. There was often a marked increase in anxiety. This showed itself in a couple of ways:

The first was *dependency*. When things become uncertain and people start to think their role is challenged, the group starts looking (usually upwards) for a leader or leaders to make the insecurity go away. This almost childlike behaviour makes the group seek certainty from above and makes any challenge to the received way of seeing and thinking even less likely.

The second was *fight or flight*. Sometimes the fighting reaction can be useful in channelling attention towards combating a tough situation. But fighting can also be internal, between teams or within the team. This reduces the capacity of the team to address the real work of understanding and responding to the real challenge, and instead makes it focus on the internal battlegrounds and blame games.

Alternatively, people can flee, disengaging from the situation, keeping their heads down and getting unnaturally interested in their spreadsheets. Looking busy is a great response to anxiety. But this isn't busyness with the real work of addressing the situation. Instead it is the busyness of playing safe and opting out of the risk. Either way the amount of brain power and attention directed to the real problem takes a dive.

The psychologist Irving Janis looked at similar situations (groups under pressure) and came up with the concept of Groupthink. Groupthink happens when group members exert pressure on group members (and outsiders) towards uniformity. It is most common where groups are highly cohesive and where there is a forceful, dominant leadership.

A really old idea

We started with Maslow, and commented that his was an 'old model'. Actually, the things we've been talking about here are much older than that.

The Buddha taught much of this 2500 years ago. He spent fifty years teaching self-examination to help his students notice how they all tended to get trapped in their beliefs, stuck in patterns of security and greed, in believing and opposing, and in generally not really seeing how things are – not having their minds open to what was actually going on.

The most important part of leading in turbulent circumstances is to really turn up here and now, paying attention to the stuck patterns of individual and group thinking that can get in the way of seeing things how they really are, and weaving new possibilities from that.

4 THE ORGANISATIONAL OBSTACLES

Whenever you do this work you will come up against external obstacles as well as inner ones. These can take many forms, but we find that certain types occur again and again.

The list below is not exhaustive. Nor are the categories totally rigid and exclusive: issues can cut across items on it. It will not produce the complete answer to everything. But we feel it's a great starting point.

- Stuck certainties
- Frosted lenses
- Unspeakables
- False harmony
- Strategy thinking that's too small.

Stuck certainties

The strongest organisations with the strongest cultures and the most perfect systems might seem the ones least in need of change. This is an illusion. They are actually among the most vulnerable to getting stuck. They get stuck in their success story.

If people in such organisations raise a question about how things are done, they are very likely to get responses like "But that's how we do it! It's part of who we are"… "It's our success formula"… "That's exactly what our customers love!"… "That's why we're number 1."

This is like the difficulty of the fish seeing the water.

We were asked to work with a large, very successful insurance company. The CEO explained why he had asked us in. "We're complacent. My top team always tend to think that everything is great, even though I don't." He carried on: "In the Budget we've just had, the rules of our part of the insurance game changed, literally overnight. The day after the Budget, our biggest competitor introduced new products responding to these new regulations. We had absolutely nothing. Our competitor had obviously been thinking about different scenarios for weeks, if not months. We hadn't. We cannot let this happen again." He went on to explain that, while his top team were no longer looking quite so sure of themselves, he wanted to make sure that their shock was translated into tangible differences.

The CEO had already noted that the company's top 30 executives were very similar: predominantly male, they were all white, middle-aged and similarly educated. But the problems went deeper. They had stopped paying attention to what was going on in the world around them. They had become strategically blind to the possibility of new risks and challenges from elsewhere.

The head of a global pharmaceutical company, with market-leading patents in its field, felt the same concern. We were asked to observe their strategy process as it brought together its country managers to think together about its international ambitions, using data collected by the central strategy team. We heard many conversations about customers, about the market they were operating in, about competitors, about external dynamics and internal capabilities. There was some excellent analytical work done. But when we asked the group what data might be missing, they found it much harder to say. Like many leading companies, they found it hard to imagine the world from a radically different position. What if their biggest danger was to come from a company very different to themselves?

We later found out that, at the same time as these managers were meeting in their swanky hotel in the sun, the founders of a small entrepreneurial pharmaceutical start-up were sitting in a cramped office plotting how to oust this market leader from its perch.

Sometimes it's not your existing competitors that are your biggest threat, and it can take an act of real imagination to see where a totally new kind of challenge might arise.

However, this kind of dangerous certainty is not only found in organisations who are leaders in their field, or at the top of organisations. Think about the comments at the beginning of this section ("But that's how we do it!"). Be honest, how often have you heard these or something similar said where you work, at every level too, not just in the boardroom but round the water cooler and the coffee machine? How often have you heard yourself saying something along those lines?

It is good for an organisation to have a strong identity towards which people can gravitate and in which they can feel pride. But this becomes an issue when that organisation can't see how something outside their identity might be an opportunity or a threat.

Frosted lenses

Lenses help us see the world. In microscopes they enable us to see items invisible to the naked eye. Lenses in telescopes bring us the wonders of the planets and of stars hundreds and thousands of light years away. The lenses of reading glasses help millions focus on what's in front of them on the page or the screen.

However lenses can also obscure or bias perception. This is particularly true if we use the term metaphorically, to cover all the things we use to perceive the world. Our own specific lenses – our ways of seeing – are influenced by our experiences, by the language we use to talk about things, and by the imagery and metaphors we find ourselves using. Some of these can work in ways that don't always help us.

People use metaphors because organisations – and what goes on within them – are often difficult to put directly into words. This is useful as a shorthand, which makes a lot of sense and saves detailed explanation every time someone opens their mouth.

Common organisational metaphors are:

- *Mechanical*: 'cogs in the machine', 'slamming on the brake', 'putting a spanner in the works', 'stepping up a gear', 'the engine room', 'pulling the right lever', 'chains of command'.
- *Organic*: 'green shoots', 'fresh growth', or the more brutal 'dead wood', 'root and branch change'.
- *Military*: 'must-win battles', 'arming the troops', 'taking the high ground'.
- *Family*: from the very explicit 'we are all one family' (usually where this is used, you later find that 'we' are anything but – and we'll come back to this later) to the more obscure 'black sheep' or 'ugly stepsister'.

There is nothing inherently right or wrong about the use of any of these metaphors, but each of them is an example of a lens. As such, they can be helpful; they put something in a context and make it easy for others to understand messages. But each lens also fixes a way of seeing, and that closes off options and potential alternative contexts or interpretations.

In organisations, the lenses that everyone looks through can become frosted and stuck, and this has consequences in the way they think about leadership, power, strategy, roles, relationships, and a host of other topics. The choice or – more powerful still – the unconscious use of metaphors (and all the images that flow from them) is full of meaning and importance. We want to encourage everyone to pay attention to the language and imagery they find in use, and which they find themselves using. Nothing in this way of speaking or imagery is value-neutral and each one brings with it its own limitations and consequences.

Take the machine metaphor, for example. What kind of leadership does the machine narrative invite? What does it imply about everyone else? If the machine has a driver, what roles are available for the rest of the people?

We have often heard senior leadership teams say, "We've got a great strategy, but we can't get people to buy in. They just won't step up. What can we do?" Often, when we dig a bit deeper, we find that the organisation is full of machine language. The machine metaphor finds an expression in machine behaviour. Did you ever find the cogs in a machine throwing their hearts and minds into driving it?

At other times, messages get mixed. Often we find that an organisation is asking people to be both cogs and humans, accelerator pedals and passionate human beings serving a purpose.

Lenses can give rise to stories that become fixed. In one very entrepreneurial organisation, the dominant story was all about the power of the founder, Bob. "It's Bob's train set", people said, "ultimately it's his call on everything." When any one story becomes the dominant (or even the only) lens, this can lead to the organisation becoming very stuck in one way of seeing things. The people in Bob's business never brought him any idea unless they were sure he'd like it. Challenging Bob's view of the world was impossible.

Bob liked alpha-male leaders who wowed customers to maximise sales. He loved to tell celebration stories about heroic performance, often involving one super-performer he dubbed 'Golden Balls' – a talented young salesman who was allowed to write his own rules, as long as he delivered the sales figures. Everyone loves success and celebration, but there's a shadow side to such narrative. If success only looks like 'Golden Balls', what are the consequences for diversity? What about other less charismatic but different ways of winning and keeping customers? No one in this business would have actively wanted to block different kinds of leaders, but there was no doubt that the legend of 'Golden Balls' had a dominant effect that led to the company having a very male culture.

One management consultancy we worked with had a very sales-driven ethos – sales growth was the biggest story in town. To deliver results, the activities involved in selling projects became separated out from responsibility for the delivery of them. The sales teams focused on selling as much work as they could, hitting their targets. The delivery teams struggled with the extra work this brought in – they either needed more people or more time. Things came to a head when the firm realised it was four weeks away from not being able to meet its payroll requirements.

It is also natural to have lenses that frame 'our market', 'our customers' and 'our suppliers'. Below is an example.

If you're over 40, you'll remember the furniture shops that used to be in the high street. Maybe your parents took you to one to buy a new sofa. You'll probably remember a stuffy atmosphere with lots of sofas lined up, of different styles but nearly all of them variations on beige, brown or orange. The staff would help you make a choice. Your parents might look through swatches of fabric, choosing which one the sofa was going to be covered with. You didn't take the sofa home with you; it would be delivered 6-8 weeks later.

This was all part of the DNA of the traditional family-run furniture shop. Every town had this kind of outlet. The formula was based on a fixed group of rules about what was needed to be successful: have a high street location; have great choices of styles of furniture made by top quality manufacturers; have good choices of fabric; and offer really reliable delivery times so that people know when their sofa is going to arrive (albeit 2–3 months away). This was all part of the lens through which such businesses saw themselves, and how they measured themselves and made decisions. 'Is our location good enough?' 'Who are the best manufacturers?' 'Who produces the best fabrics?'

IKEA changed all this. The things that made the traditional furniture shop successful, the things that the people who ran those shops believed were crucial to their customers – this 'deep recipe' – was completely reversed by IKEA. In IKEA, furniture is more of a fashion item. You don't see sofas lined up with other sofas; you see rooms set up. The furniture is usually available to take home with you that day. It isn't expected to last a lifetime. The shop isn't on the high street; you drive to it as a destination, a venue where you can eat meatballs and the kids can play. There are queues outside IKEA on a Sunday, of people going for a day out.

There are many other examples of such a shift of lens. Think about the airlines that have cut out all the frills to deliver the lowest cost – shifting the fixed lens view of what an airline should provide. Think about all the online offers, from book sales to dating, from renting a room to calling a taxi – each one of them arising from a willingness to change the lens through which a business is seen. In each case the possibility remains invisible unless, and until, you have a shift of lens.

Ask yourself what is the 'deep recipe' for your business? What is it you assume that your customers most value and most want you to do? Then ask which of these ingredients might be too small, or maybe even limiting and dangerous to you? What different business would you get if you tweaked or even reversed the recipe?

Unspeakables

There will be some things you really cannot say out loud in your organisation – these are the 'unspeakables'.

A number of years ago we were working with senior managers in a consumer business about how they could think more creatively about future opportunities. As part of this conversation we moved on to talking about obstacles that might get in the way of this future focus. Ideas flowed and soon we had a flipchart full of them. Then one manager spoke up. "Of course, you realise that there are quite a few things on that list that we can't actually say in public."

At the end of the workshop, the group asked what would happen to the flipchart. "It needs to go in the bin!" said someone. They meant it, too. The flipchart was not only torn up and binned, but the bits were pushed to the bottom of the bin. That's how unspeakable a number of things were in that company.

Why is this? It's like that ancient story of the Emperor and his new clothes. Having been persuaded by two deceitful weavers that he had been made a beautiful set of new clothes that would be invisible to those who were stupid or incompetent, the Emperor paraded naked down the street. He could see that he was naked, the crowds gathered to see him could see that he was naked, yet nobody said anything. The Emperor didn't comment on his nakedness as he believed it was his own stupidity or inadequacy that meant he couldn't see his new clothes in all their splendour. The crowd were too scared to speak up.

An entrepreneur we know set up a FinTech company many years ago. "Every decision goes through me," he proudly said. But over the years, as the company got bigger and bigger, this wasn't possible. Yet the founder continued to tell his 'hands on' story to new joiners, to suppliers, to customers. The staff knew that this couldn't continue yet were scared of telling the boss. Even his management team fudged the issue in regular meetings until, over time, the topic of the founder's hands-on decision-making became something one could not mention. Instead people worked around it, duplicating effort where necessary and spending more time than was needed, all to fulfil this myth.

Like the crowds that silently lined the streets watching their naked Emperor walk past, the employees of the company played along with the myth and said nothing. The truth had become unspeakable.

False harmony

"We're just one big happy family." We've already talked about family metaphor and here's another example. But are 'we' really? Would it even be a good thing to be so harmonious anyway?

False harmony is possibly the greatest enemy of the types of relationships needed for genuine collaboration. Organisations can place a huge premium on the pretence that everyone is 'in the same boat' or 'singing from the same hymn sheet' (or whatever cliché they prefer). This can then be used as a way of silencing all curiosity, all questions and all disagreement.

Whilst it's great to have constructive relationships where people get along, it's no good if this hides genuine disagreements that need to be explored.

A financial brokerage firm based in the City of London was privately-owned, and had long been the fiefdom of its owner and chief executive. After many years at the helm, Mr Norman – as the staff called him – decided to retire and sell his company. Negotiations were held with a very large organisation and terms agreed to everyone's satisfaction. Mr Norman would get his money and the buyer would complement its existing service with new lines of business.

But it didn't work out like that. While Mr Norman bought himself a very large yacht, the acquiror failed to get the results it had anticipated.

While carrying out their due diligence, the directors of the acquiror had heard stories, but ignored them, considering them merely quaint. They had heard how only

Mr Norman was allowed to adjust the paintings on the wall if they were slightly askew; how managers and directors had to stand every time Mr Norman came into the room; how the second most powerful person in the company was his secretary. These turned out not to be quaint at all, but to reveal the reality of the firm: passivity, fear of doing or saying anything that might be seen as challenging the status quo, unwillingness to take responsibility.

So beware if you hear an organisation boast that "We never have arguments… we all really like each other." This is often hiding important conversations that are being suppressed, either consciously or unconsciously. False harmony will get in the way of the creativity, innovation, new thinking and questioning that may be essential.

Strategy thinking that's too small

In most organisations, strategic thinking and business planning take the form of a ritual. Often the same people are involved every year, the same external consultants, the same process, the same timings. It may even involve filling in the same pieces of paper.

It doesn't have to be that way. It's worth getting curious about what is possible in your strategic thinking and business planning.

Very frequently, strategic thinking and business planning is purely analytical. You're asked to fill in tables, give estimates, prepare budgets, analyse prices. These are valuable activities, but if you think about how great products and new services come about, they don't usually come solely from this activity. They come from creativity and innovation. How many shops selling 60 cent refillable coffees would you have to analyse before you invented Starbucks? How many traditional taxi firms before you imagined Uber?

Strategy can't solely be an analytical act. It is really important not to let your view of strategy become too small to do the job. You need a bigger approach: one with enough creative input, with sufficient and rigorous challenges to received wisdom, with deliberate and open-eyed processes for finding the unseen angles and hearing the unheard voices.

Strategy is often the preserve of the CEO, or maybe the board. It could and should be more – keeping the strategic thinking to a tight team can be speedy but also runs the risk of missing out on the wider insight and market knowledge that exists in the organisation. Involving a wider group of people in strategic thinking can feel unruly to some control-hungry leaders (like Bob). But it's vital to see wider than even the most talented small team can.

Once formulated, strategy can be all too readily set in stone. Some of the most famous strategy models tell you that the more you line up your different parts of the business with your strategic objectives, the stronger you are. But we all need to remember that if you have a perfectly aligned business model where your strategy, your systems, your values, your people, your skills all line up perfectly to suit the world as it is right now, there will be terrific pressure against changing anything. Yet you may have to. The practices and tips in this book are here to help you to do this well.

So, there we have it, five reasons why attempts at change fail: stuck certainties, frosted lenses, unspeakables, false harmony, strategy thinking that's too small.

You may find your organisation is mercifully free of some but troubled by others. You might find totally different ones that are particularly important in your context.

5 A NEVER-ENDING FRONTIER

We said this book is about something bigger than a crisis response to a virus, and it is. The virus is a massive existential threat. But it isn't the only one, and it may not be the biggest or the most dangerous. We are in a world where, if we choose to look keenly, we can see that we face wave after wave of disruption across the inter-woven network of systems on which our life and societies depend. We live in a time of massive risk, challenge and threat. And of course, as it always has done, every wave of challenge brings its own frontier of possibility and opportunity.

We are a confused and complex species, polluting and salvaging, waging war and saving life. We are drawn towards comfort and security, lulling ourselves to hold onto the familiar and comfortable for just that bit too long. But at the same time, change is also woven into us. Humans have often challenged the status quo, broken free and caused changes that really made a difference. Disruption is part of what makes us human, and the frontiers for this activity are probably broader now than they have ever been. American politicians once feared that the ending of the physical frontier would blunt the spirit of innovation. It didn't, because the physical frontier was replaced by commercial and technological ones. The only limitation on our capacity to challenge and bring about beneficial change is the limitation we place on ourselves. Disruption is endless in its potential because we humans are endlessly curious, filled with energy and passion for crafting our world for the better.

Our capacity for reflection and inquiry makes such ambition possible and reasonable. All of us can play our part in keeping life, society, our organisations and institutions alive and fit for the future. We can do this because we are drawn to participate, to join in and imagine something better. Sure, we are a species that often gets this wrong. We can veer down blind allies of closed minds and false certainty, and deny our capacity for curiosity, sharing and learning. It takes the discipline of the positive disruptor and the practice of inquiry to keep us alive and alert at the frontier.

We end right back with the oldest stories, because they contain the most current wisdom. We are looking at the future in the good company of the Buddha, who said, "Pay attention to your mind, your body, your delusions." It's easy to crave certainty and cling to the familiar when something more impermanent and flexible might serve us much better. "Wake up, don't be deluded," the Buddha also said. Of course, we often get this wrong and fall short. Even the best of us falls and falters, he tells us. But every day we begin again. That is as close to a truth as we can find. As long as we have the will and the passion to do it, every day we begin again. The frontier always lies ahead, unmapped and ever beckoning.

ACKNOWLEDGEMENTS

We've been working in this field for more than twenty years and have had the privilege of training with some of the legends of the organisational consulting field. Their wisdom has helped us to shape our work, and is woven through all that we do and all that we create. Some of the work has been specifically credited in the text of our book, but many more people have played a role in shaping our practice. We want to acknowledge all of them.

We learned massively from our time working in the pioneering firm Ashridge Consulting. Our colleagues and clients over many years played a huge role in developing our practice. We also pay tribute to Bill Critchley, Caryn Vanstone, Kathleen King, Hugh Pidgeon, Kamil Kellner who were Chris's teachers on the Ashridge MSc in Organisational Consulting many years ago, and to our fellow directors on the Ashridge Consulting leadership team, where we learned much about leading emergent consulting practices.

We thank all those in the worldwide community of practice whose ideas we have drawn on in our work. Bill Torbert, Ralph Stacey, Patricia Shaw, David Cooperrider and colleagues at Case Western, and the CARPP team at Bath, Peter Reason, Judi Marshall, Gill Coleman, have especially informed our work. We also thank the Ashridge MSc in Sustainability and Responsibility team, including our dear and sadly late colleague Dr Chris Seeley.

Beyond this we applaud our clients from over the years as well as our colleagues at GameShift, who are our helpers in moving forward the frontier of practice, creating the emerging future of organisations as we explore together to create the new world. We have learnt enormous amounts from each and every one of you in so many different ways.

And for everyone we have been unable to name in these acknowledgements, thank you for being part of our journey and our learning.

We'd also like to thank Chris West for his skills, and patience, as a writing coach.

Finally, to our long-suffering families and friends, who have put up with the consequences of our itinerant consulting lifestyles for decades, we offer our apologies and gratitude.

Chris & Philippa

ABOUT THE AUTHORS

Philippa Hardman and Chris Nichols met at Ashridge Consulting where they jointly led the Strategy Engagement practice before joining the Leadership Team as directors of Performance and Innovation respectively. Both come from financial backgrounds – Chris as an investment banker in New York and Price Waterhouse practice leader in Australia, and Philippa as a Chartered Accountant, qualifying with PwC in London.

The focus of their work together has been to harness the power of creative participative processes in organisational life. They have breathed new life into strategic conversations, crafting ways for top management teams to stimulate totally new conversations, see the world differently and bring new actions to life. Their work has spanned the UK and Europe, North America and Asia, and continues today in helping their clients continue to address their most significant challenges in fresh ways.

They set up GameShift to continue and expand this work. GameShift is a niche collaborative consultancy which focuses on bringing about purposeful and radical change by helping people to work together rigorously, creatively and practically. Philippa, Chris and the wider GameShift team are delighted that their work has been recognised by peers and clients by being voted onto the FT Leading Management Consultants' listing for the last three years and, in 2019, GameShift was a finalist in the Leadership Development category of the Training Journal awards for its work with the Danish health and medical system.